FEARFUL

TO

FEARLESS

YOUR JOURNEY FROM
FEAR TO **FREEDOM**

WRITTEN BY
MIKE JENSEN

LiveLife**Happy** Publishing

Library of Congress Cataloging-in-Publication Data

Mike Jensen

Fearful To Fearless

Categories: Self-Help > Personal Transformation > Psychology > Emotions & Mental Health > Business & Money > Motivational Management & Leadership

ISBN Paperback 978-1-998724-04-8

ISBN Digital 978-1-998724-05-5

Cover Design: Mike Jensen

Live Life Happy Publishing

PUBLISHER'S NOTE & AUTHOR DISCLAIMER

This publication is designed to provide accurate and authoritative information concerning the subject matter covered. It is sold to understand that the publisher and author are not engaging in or rendering any psychological, medical or other professional services. If expert assistance or counselling is needed, seek the services of a competent medical professional. For immediate support call your local crisis line. The following book could contain actual events and experiences that the author has encountered in their life. However, some names and specific locations have been changed or omitted to protect the privacy and confidentiality of the individuals involved. The changes do not alter the story's integrity or its messages.

Dedication

To my wife, Stacey—my fearless guiding light. From the moment we met at age nine, you were unafraid to be yourself, embracing this rough country boy without hesitation. In high school, you wore confidence like a crown, walking through the halls with a strength that inspired me. As a new mother, you brought grace and patience, learning to understand our three boys and the wonder of their growing personalities. And despite your own fears, you traveled the country on your own, tackling every journey with resilience. Today, as a grandmother and the powerhouse behind a billion-dollar company, you lead with unwavering courage. Your strength in the face of fear has been my greatest inspiration, guiding me to discover my own courage. Thank you for being my fearless anchor and shining light.

TABLE OF CONTENT

INTRODUCTION

Welcome to Your Journey
from Fearful to Fearless

Embracing the Reality of Fear

"Have you ever felt like fear controls your life? Maybe it's a fear of failure, of rejection, or of stepping outside your comfort zone. If so, you're not alone."

Right from the start, we want readers to know they're in good company and that fear is a universal experience. By normalizing fear, we set a compassionate, understanding tone that encourages readers to feel comfortable and open to change.

Interestingly, we are only born with two innate fears: the fear of loud noises and the fear of falling. Every other fear we have is learned—passed down through experiences with others or events in our lives. These learned fears arise from beliefs we adopt, often without realizing it, and they shape how we perceive and interact with the world. This means that fear, while powerful, is something we've developed, and therefore, it's something we can reshape.

The Purpose of This Book

"This book is not about eliminating fear completely—that would be impossible, and honestly, a bit unnatural. Instead, it's about learning to live with fear in a way that allows you to feel free, confident, and in control. It's about transforming fear from a roadblock into a companion that helps you grow."

Here, we introduce the concept of working with fear rather than against it, setting a realistic expectation. We clarify that the goal is not a "fear-free life" but rather a fearless approach to life's challenges.

Why Fear Exists and Why We All Have It

Let's take a moment to explain the basic idea that fear is a protective mechanism—one that's been with us since the beginning of humanity. But in today's world, our fears are often more mental and abstract.

Imagine, for instance, that ancient fear of facing a predator. Today, our "predators" might look more like failure, judgment, or loss. Our minds have the same reactions to these modern "threats," even though they don't pose the same immediate physical danger. Adding to this is the fact that many of our fears were learned through experiences or others' influence. What once served as a protective mechanism can now feel like a barrier holding us back. But with the right tools, we can reframe and manage these fears effectively.

Setting Out on the Path:
What You'll Learn in This Book

The book will be a guide through four key phases of transformation:

Understanding Fear: You'll learn where fear comes from, how it affects you, and the difference between real, immediate fears and imagined ones that arise from worry and anxiety.

Embracing Fear: Rather than avoiding or pushing fear away, you'll discover ways to accept and even welcome it as a motivator for growth. You'll see that fear can guide you toward meaningful experiences and connections.

Processing Fear: This section will help you shift out of "survival mode," where fear keeps you stuck, and into "creation mode," where you can approach life from a place of excitement and possibility.

Practicing Fearlessness: Finally, you'll gain practical tools and steps to live more courageously, building resilience and confidence one small step at a time.

A Personal Invitation

"I invite you to see this book as a personal journey, not a set of rules. You don't have to rush or feel like you need to 'fix' yourself. Instead, take each chapter as a chance to get to know yourself better, to build a life where fear doesn't hold you back but instead inspires you to live fully."

A First Step: Acknowledge Your Fears

Before diving into the book, we can suggest a simple first exercise. "Take a few moments to reflect on one or two fears that have been on your mind. What areas of your life do they impact? Write them down somewhere safe. This small step is a powerful start, as acknowledging our fears is the first step toward understanding them."

CHAPTER 1

ACKNOWLEDGING FEAR

Understanding and Confronting Our Deepest Emotions

Fear: Why Do We Feel It?

"Fear." Just saying the word can make you feel tense.

But have you ever thought about what fear actually is?

Why does it show up in our lives, and why does it feel so powerful?

Fear is an ancient emotion, one of our most basic survival tools. Imagine our ancestors navigating a dangerous world, filled with wild animals and treacherous landscapes. For them, fear was a signal to pay attention. It would spark that immediate, gut-level reaction to fight, flee, or freeze—whatever it took to stay alive.

In the modern world, however, we rarely face immediate life-or-death situations. Our dangers look different now: we fear things like failure, social judgment, financial insecurity, and even loneliness. But our bodies and brains still react as if we're under direct physical threat, which can make ordinary challenges feel overwhelming. When you're anxious before a big presentation or social event, that pounding heart, shallow breath, and shaky hands are actually your body's way of saying, "Watch out! Danger ahead."

Understanding fear as a natural, built-in response is a great first step toward taking powerful influence over it. Instead of seeing it as an enemy, we can start to see it as a reaction that, while uncomfortable, is deeply human.

The Role of Fear in Modern Life

Think about a typical day. How often do you feel even a little bit nervous, tense, or worried? Fear shows up in many forms, from the subtle anxiety of making a tough decision to the intense dread of public speaking or facing a big life change.

Today's world also magnifies fear. With the constant news about financial downturns, health scares, and global issues, it's easy to feel on edge all the time. This constant exposure can push us into what's called "survival mode," a state where fear keeps us always alert and defensive.

In survival mode, our brains are wired to scan for threats, which limits our ability to think clearly and enjoy life. Have you ever noticed feeling irritable or distracted after watching a tense news segment? Or unable to focus because of a worry that keeps spinning in your mind? That's survival mode at work. When we're stuck here, fear dominates, using up our energy and leaving us with little room for creativity, relaxation, or connection.

Types of Fear: Reality-Based vs. Imaginative

There are two main types of fear, and knowing the difference can help you understand how to respond to each.

1. Reality-Based Fear (Physical Fear)
Reality-based fear is an instinctual reaction to real, immediate danger. For instance, if you were walking in the woods and saw a snake on the path, your body would respond in seconds. Your

heart would race, your muscles would tighten, and adrenaline would surge through your system. This is reality-based fear—your mind and body working together to keep you safe.

Similarly, standing at the edge of a cliff without a railing can make you feel light-headed and cautious. This fear is a natural warning to be careful, rooted in the present and grounded in a real physical threat. Our fear of heights, deep water, or fast moving cars are examples of reality-based fear. This type of fear is valuable; it helps us avoid situations that could harm us.

2. Imaginative Fear (Mental Fear)
Imaginative fear, on the other hand, is different. It doesn't come from a direct physical threat but from the stories our minds create about what might happen. Picture yourself preparing for a big presentation at work. You've practiced, you know your material, but still, thoughts start creeping in: "What if I forget everything? What if I embarrass myself?"

These "what if" fears aren't based on reality but on imagined scenarios that your mind plays out. They're based on possibilities, not facts, yet they can feel just as real and intense. Imaginative fear can be powerful because it often holds us back from taking action, growing, and pursuing our goals. It's this kind of fear that can make us avoid social situations, stay in unfulfilling jobs, or turn down new opportunities.

How Fear Can Limit Us

Both types of fear have their place in our lives. Reality-based fear keeps us safe in the face of true danger, and imaginative fear can sometimes stop us from making reckless decisions. But when left unchecked, fear can also limit us from living up to our potential.

Impact of Reality-Based Fears

If we let physical fear take control, it can prevent us from experiencing life fully. Think of someone with a fear of flying. Despite air travel being statistically safe, this fear may prevent them from visiting family or exploring new places. It becomes a barrier to opportunities for joy and connection.

The Hold of Mental Fears

Mental fear rooted in "what if" thinking, can trap us in a cycle of hesitation and missed opportunities. When we focus too much on imagined worst-case scenarios, we stop seeing the present possibilities. Fear of failure, for instance, often keeps people from pursuing dreams or taking steps toward a fulfilling career. In holding onto these fears, we limit ourselves and our potential.

Breaking Free from Fear:

The Power of Acknowledgment

The first step to overcoming any kind of fear is to acknowledge it. When we ignore fear, it doesn't go away. Instead, it lurks in the background, subtly influencing our actions and decisions.

Imagine fear as a shadow in a dark room. The more you avoid looking at it, the more intimidating it feels. But when you turn on the light and face it, the shadow becomes less threatening. Similarly, when you acknowledge fear, you give yourself the power to examine it and respond thoughtfully.

Take a moment to think about a fear you've been avoiding. Maybe it's the fear of making a big change, like switching careers, or the fear of speaking in front of others. Acknowledging this fear doesn't mean it disappears instantly, but it does mean you're ready to start managing it.

Understanding Limiting Beliefs and Irrational Fears

Imaginative fear is often intensified by two things: limiting beliefs and irrational fears.

Limiting Beliefs

Limiting beliefs are typically born from early experiences and reinforced over time. They often start as external judgments or societal norms imposed by others—family, friends, teachers, or society. When we hear things like, "You're not good at math," "You're too shy to be a leader," or even subtler messages like, "People like us don't do that," we start to internalize these as truths. These statements might not be rooted in reality, but they're powerful because they come from sources we trust or respect, making them seem valid or even indisputable.

Once these messages take hold, they begin to shape our self-perception. We absorb these external assessments and adopt them as part of our identity. Over time, they transform from mere suggestions or criticisms into our own beliefs, rooted deeply in our subconscious.

The mind, in an attempt to protect us, starts to filter experiences through the lens of these beliefs, reinforcing them every time we encounter situations that seem to "prove" them right. For example, if you've adopted the belief "I'm not good at meeting new people" because of a few awkward experiences, you might start to avoid situations where you'd have to socialize. Each time you do, it reinforces the belief, creating a cycle of avoidance and confirmation.

Interestingly, these beliefs can become so embedded that we don't even question them; they feel like facts about ourselves rather than choices or opinions. They become "self-fulfilling prophecies," shaping our lives in ways that limit our potential. This is why they're so tricky to overcome: because they don't feel like barriers we've put up—they feel like the boundaries of who we are.

Irrational Fears

Irrational fears, also known as "phobias" or "unfounded fears," are fears that exist despite a clear understanding that they lack a rational basis. They are often rooted in exaggerated perceptions of danger, causing distress even when the individual knows logically that the fear is unwarranted. These fears are different from rational fears, which are grounded in real threats or legitimate concerns. By learning to recognize and confront irrational fears, we can begin to approach them with objectivity, treating them as mental obstacles instead of true risks.

Examples of Irrational Fears and How They Manifest:

1.   Fear of Flying

Many people experience a fear of flying even though statistics repeatedly show it's one of the safest forms of travel. This fear often stems from a sense of losing control or an exaggerated perception of danger in the air. An individual might logically understand that flying is safe but still experience sweaty palms, rapid heartbeat, or even panic at the thought of boarding a plane. Acknowledging this fear as irrational can allow them to examine the underlying thoughts, such as "I have no control" or "What if something goes wrong?" and reframe these into more balanced perspectives.

2.   Fear of Public Speaking

Public speaking is another common irrational fear. Although no physical harm is associated with speaking in front of others, many people feel an intense fear of embarrassment, judgment, or failure. This fear can prevent someone from advancing in their career or sharing valuable ideas. Recognizing it as an irrational fear can help a person understand that their fear is more about the discomfort of vulnerability rather than an actual danger.

3.   Fear of Rejection

Fear of rejection often arises in social settings, relationships, or professional environments. For instance, someone might avoid asking for a promotion or expressing romantic interest because they fear being turned down. This fear can become irrational when it prevents someone from pursuing meaningful opportunities based on the assumption that rejection equates to failure or personal inadequacy. By viewing rejection as a natural part of life rather than a defining judgment, one can start to loosen the hold of this fear.

4.   Fear of Germs or Contamination

Some people experience an intense fear of germs (known as "germaphobia") that goes beyond reasonable caution. They may avoid touching doorknobs, using public restrooms, or shaking hands to an extreme degree, even when they logically understand that ordinary hygiene practices should suffice. This fear, often linked to a need for control or an amplified sense of personal vulnerability, can be managed by gradually building tolerance and trust in appropriate cleanliness measures.

How Irrational Fears Develop:

Irrational fears often stem from early experiences, conditioning, or even past traumatic events that create an exaggerated mental association between certain situations and danger. They're reinforced by our brain's natural tendency to avoid discomfort or perceived threats, leading us to avoid these situations altogether. For instance, if someone experienced a turbulent flight or witnessed someone else have a public speaking mishap, the brain might lock in a belief that such situations are threatening, creating a heightened response in the future.

Once these fears are established, they become self-perpetuating. Every time we avoid a feared situation, the brain receives a signal that it was a good decision, reinforcing the irrational belief. This cycle strengthens the mental association between the situation and a perceived danger, making the fear feel more real.

Conclusion

Moving Forward with Awareness

Acknowledging fear—whether physical or mental—is a powerful, transformative first step. It's a way of saying, "I see you, fear, but you don't control me." By recognizing fear as a natural part of life, you open the door to understanding it and learning to live with it.

As we move forward, you'll learn how embracing fear rather than resisting it can be a pathway to personal growth. By seeing fear not as an obstacle but as a guide, you can take the first steps toward living a fuller, more fearless life.

Reflection Exercise: Getting to Know Your Fear

Take a moment to think about a fear you've been carrying.

Write it down, and then ask yourself:

1. Is this a physical fear, something based on a real threat?

2. Or is it an imaginative fear, something based on a "what if" scenario?

By identifying and acknowledging the type of fear, you've already taken the first step toward understanding and managing it. Embrace this moment—it's the beginning of your journey from fearful to fearless.

CHAPTER 2

EMBRACING FEAR

The Power of Acceptance
as a Path to Growth

Changing How We See Fear

Most of us naturally view fear as an enemy, something we'd rather avoid or eliminate. When fear shows up, our instinct is to push it away, hoping it will disappear. But imagine what could happen if, instead of running from fear, we learned to accept and even embrace it.

Think about a time you were on the verge of doing something important—a big decision, a new relationship, or even a significant personal goal. Often, fear shows up at these critical moments not as a warning, but as a sign that you're about to grow or change. In this chapter, we'll explore how embracing fear rather than resisting it can open doors to opportunities and help us live a more expansive life.

Section 1: Real-Life Examples of Embracing Fear

Throughout history, many people who achieved great success have learned to embrace fear and use it as fuel for their achievements. Here are a few relatable examples of how individuals have used fear as a catalyst for growth:

Athletes: Professional athletes, for instance, often feel a rush of fear before competitions. They know they're about to face a challenge that requires their absolute best, which can be intimidating. But instead of letting that fear paralyze them, they use it to heighten their focus and energy, channeling it into their performance.

Entrepreneurs: Starting a business is one of the most uncertain paths someone can take. Entrepreneurs frequently face fear of failure, loss, and uncertainty. Instead of being held back, successful entrepreneurs use this fear as a motivator to prepare thoroughly, strategize, and develop resilience. For them, fear is a reminder of what's at stake and a prompt to stay alert and adaptable.

These examples remind us that fear can actually push us to reach our fullest potential. Rather than holding us back, fear can be the spark that lights the way forward.

Section 2: Seeing Fear as a Guide

One of the most empowering ways to change your relationship with fear is to view it as a guide. Fear often arises when we step outside our comfort zones, signaling that we're on the edge of growth.

Think of fear as a compass—it points us toward experiences that have the potential to shape us, to teach us something new, or to expand our horizons.

Everyday Examples of Fear as a Guide

Pursuing a New Job: Imagine you're considering a new job that's outside your comfort zone. You feel fear because you worry about meeting the new responsibilities. But this fear doesn't mean you should avoid the opportunity; rather, it could mean the role has the potential to help you grow. Embracing that fear may open up new skills, confidence, and achievements you didn't think possible.

Starting a New Relationship: The beginning of a new relationship can bring up all sorts of vulnerabilities. You might fear being hurt or bringing in past baggage. But this fear also signals that this connection has the potential to bring joy and meaning if you're willing to lean in and face it.

Learning a New Skill: Think of a time when you wanted to try something new, like speaking a new language or taking up a hobby, but felt afraid of failing. This fear signals that you're challenging yourself and stepping into unfamiliar territory. Embracing it allows you to grow, learn, and experience the satisfaction of developing a new skill.

In all these cases, fear isn't something to avoid. Instead, it's a tool for growth, a natural reaction that encourages us to expand beyond what's comfortable.

Section 3: Practical Ways to Embrace Fear

Now that we understand that fear can be a guide, let's explore ways to actively embrace it in daily life. Here are a few practical techniques:

1. Name Your Fear
The first step in embracing fear is acknowledging it directly. When fear arises, rather than ignoring it, give it a name. For instance, if you feel nervous about a job interview, try saying, "I'm feeling anxious because I want to make a good impression." Naming fear

turns it from a vague threat into something concrete that you can understand and manage.

2. Break Down Your Fear into Small Steps

Fear can feel overwhelming when faced all at once. By breaking it into smaller steps, you make it more manageable. For example, if you're afraid of swimming in deep water, start by standing in the shallow end. Then practice floating or swimming near the edge. Gradually venture a little deeper as you gain confidence. Each step helps you build trust in yourself, showing that fear can be conquered one step at a time.

3. Ask What Your Fear is Trying to Teach You

Often, fear contains valuable lessons. When you feel afraid, pause and ask yourself, "What is this fear telling me?" Maybe it's showing you that you need to prepare more, or it's highlighting an area where you need more confidence. By viewing fear as a teacher, you shift from resisting it to learning from it.

4. Practice Gratitude for Fear

This might sound unusual, but try to be grateful for your fears. Each fear you face offers an opportunity to grow stronger and wiser. Next time you encounter a challenging situation, thank your fear for showing you where you have room to grow. This mindset can transform fear from something negative into something constructive.

Changing Our Relationship with Fear

To truly embrace fear, it's important to change how we relate to it. Here are three key mindset shifts that can help:

From Avoidance to Curiosity

Approaching fear with curiosity is a powerful way to reduce its intensity and transform it from a source of anxiety into an opportunity for growth. When we're curious, we shift from a reactive mindset—where fear feels like an insurmountable barrier—to a proactive mindset, where fear becomes something we can observe, understand, and learn from. Curiosity allows us to engage with our emotions rather than running from them, making fear feel more manageable and less like a looming threat.

Curiosity takes us out of "fight-or-flight" mode and puts us into a more reflective, investigative state of mind. When we become curious, we're able to detach ourselves slightly from the emotional grip of fear, allowing us to view it from a distance. This shift in perspective helps us see fear not as something to resist, but as a natural response that might hold valuable insights about ourselves, our boundaries, or our past experiences. By asking questions about our fear, we allow ourselves to explore it gently, making it less likely that we'll feel overwhelmed.

From Resistance to Acceptance

When fear arises, our instinct is often to resist or suppress it, hoping it will disappear. But resistance typically intensifies the feeling, making the fear seem larger and more powerful than it actually is. Instead, try viewing fear as just another natural emotion—one that doesn't define or control you. Like joy, sadness, or excitement, fear is a part of the full spectrum of human experience. By acknowledging and accepting it without judgment, you can diminish its hold, allowing it to coexist without dictating your actions. Acceptance creates space for you to observe fear with curiosity rather than panic, letting you move forward alongside it, rather than battling against it. This shift in approach can transform fear from a barrier into a stepping stone toward growth and resilience.

From Fear of Failure to Love of Learning

Often, our fear comes from a fear of failure. By reframing failure as a learning opportunity, we lessen fear's hold over us. Instead of seeing mistakes as setbacks, we can view them as lessons that contribute to personal growth.

Building Confidence Through Embracing Fear

Each time we embrace fear, we build confidence. Every small step taken in the presence of fear strengthens our resilience and courage. Here are a few ways to celebrate and build confidence as you embrace fear:

Celebrate Small Wins: Every time you face a fear, no matter how small, take a moment to acknowledge it. For example, if you're afraid of networking and manage to introduce yourself to someone, that's a victory. Each small step builds confidence, making the next challenge feel less daunting.

Reflect on Past Experiences: Think back to a time when you faced a fear and came out stronger. Reflecting on these experiences reminds you that you're capable of handling difficult situations. If you were once afraid of a job interview and succeeded, use that experience to reassure yourself during new challenges.

Surround Yourself with Encouragement: Supportive people can help you embrace fear with confidence. Surround yourself with friends, family, or mentors who believe in you. Their encouragement can boost your confidence, reminding you that you don't have to face fear alone.

Conclusion

The Freedom of Embracing Fear

When we embrace fear, we free ourselves from its control. Fear no longer becomes a force that holds us back but a guide that helps us grow. By accepting fear as a natural part of the journey, we become more resilient, open to change, and willing to pursue opportunities that lead to a fuller, richer life.

Reflection Exercise: Reframing Your Fears

Take a moment to reflect on a fear that's been holding you back.

Write down:

1. What the fear is telling you about yourself.

2. What lessons you could learn by facing this fear?

3. One small, practical step you could take toward embracing this fear today.

Fear can be a powerful teacher if we're willing to listen. Embrace this reflection as a way to connect with your fear, understanding it as a guide rather than a roadblock.

CHAPTER 3
PROCESSING FEAR

Moving from Survival Mode to Creation Mode

Understanding Survival Mode and Its Effects

Fear evolved as a sophisticated survival mechanism, designed to help our ancestors respond with lightning speed to immediate threats. Imagine an ancient human encountering a wild animal—their brain instantly triggers "survival mode," releasing adrenaline and other stress hormones to prepare for fight or flight, a split-second response essential to their survival.

Today, survival mode still has its value, enabling us to stay alert in genuinely dangerous situations. However, in the modern world, this response often activates for non-life-threatening events—such as looming work deadlines, social engagements, or financial stressors. Remaining in this heightened state of vigilance for prolonged periods takes a mental and physical toll, sapping our energy and preventing us from enjoying a calm, balanced life.

In this chapter, we'll explore how to identify the signs of survival mode, examine its impact on our lives, and introduce ways to shift into a more open, relaxed "creation mode," where we can approach life's challenges thoughtfully rather than reactively.

Section 1: The Fight-or-Flight Response – What Happens in Your Body?

When we enter survival mode, our bodies undergo a series of physiological changes, automatically priming us to handle perceived threats. Although valuable in true emergencies, this response can be a barrier when it's triggered by everyday stressors. Here's a breakdown of what happens and why it matters:

Increased Heart Rate and Breathing:
The moment your brain detects a threat, it signals the release of adrenaline, accelerating your heart rate and quickening your breathing. This rush of blood to your muscles and oxygen to your brain sharpens reflexes for immediate action. While helpful in short bursts, prolonged shallow breathing and increased heart rate can lead to feelings of dizziness, tension, or panic in everyday situations, like public speaking or intense work meetings, even though these scenarios are not physically dangerous.

Stress Hormones:
Adrenaline and cortisol, the primary stress hormones, are released to heighten alertness and boost energy by flooding your bloodstream with glucose. While beneficial in the short term, prolonged cortisol exposure leads to disrupted sleep patterns, weakened immune function, and, over time, chronic fatigue or burnout. This constant exposure can leave your body struggling to shift back to a relaxed state, making it harder to recover and impacting your mental health and resilience.

Tunnel Vision:
Survival mode narrows your focus exclusively on the perceived threat, a reaction beneficial in emergencies but limiting when triggered by everyday stress. For instance, in a high-stress work environment, you may concentrate intently on immediate tasks but overlook creative ideas, long-term solutions, or the big picture. This restricted focus favors short-term safety at the ex-

pense of long-term problem-solving and innovation, reinforcing a cycle of stress.

Understanding these responses allows us to recognize survival mode for what it is—a valuable but often misplaced reaction. By identifying these signs, we can begin managing our responses more effectively and preventing unnecessary stress from taking control. Developing this awareness is the first step in cultivating strategies that calm the body, regain mental clarity, and foster a more balanced approach to challenges.

Section 2: Recognizing Survival Mode in Your Life

Identifying when you're in survival mode is essential to regaining balance and reconnecting with a sense of calm. Although survival mode is a natural response to stress, remaining in this heightened state for extended periods can have serious implications for mental and physical well-being. Here are common signs that reveal when you might be operating from survival mode:

Physical Symptoms:
Survival mode often manifests as physical symptoms, as the body remains on high alert, bracing for potential threats. You may notice tension in your shoulders, neck, or back; clenching your jaw; frequent headaches; digestive discomfort; or muscle tightness. This constant physical bracing can leave you feeling physically exhausted, even though no immediate threat is present.

Difficulty Relaxing:
In survival mode, relaxing becomes challenging. You might find that you can't "switch off" your mind, constantly ruminating on what needs to be done or fearing worst-case scenarios. Even in quiet settings, you may feel driven to stay busy or distract yourself, finding it hard to fully rest or unwind. This inability to relax is a sign that your nervous system is in overdrive and in need of restoration.

Irritability and Emotional Reactivity:
Survival mode can amplify emotional reactivity, making you more sensitive to minor stressors. You may find yourself snapping at loved ones, becoming unusually impatient, or feeling drained in social interactions. This increased irritability is a signal that you're operating from a place of vigilance, making it difficult to approach interactions with calm and consideration.

By paying attention to these signs, you can begin to make small adjustments to ease yourself out of survival mode and back into a state of equilibrium. Practicing intentional relaxation techniques, such as deep breathing, mindfulness meditation, and regular physical activity, can help you release tension and regain a sense of calm.

Section 3: Shifting from Survival Mode to Creation Mode

The opposite of survival mode is creation mode—a mindset that fosters growth, creativity, and exploration, moving beyond the limits of fear-driven thinking. In creation mode, we enter a state of calm and openness, feeling more connected to our inner potential and the world around us. Unlike survival mode, which centers on reaction and self-preservation, creation mode encourages forward-thinking, the welcoming of new ideas, and embracing the unknown as a space for growth.

Imagine you're working on a big project. In survival mode, your thoughts may dwell on deadlines, fear of failure, or concern about others' opinions. This mindset narrows your focus to what could go wrong, leaving you feeling tense and preoccupied. But in creation mode, you shift to curiosity and excitement, focusing on what you can build, the new skills you'll gain, and the relationships you'll foster. Instead of worrying, "What if I fail?" you begin to ask, "What can I achieve?" or "How can I make an impact?" This positive mindset reduces self-doubt and motivates you to give your best, broadening your perspective and allowing you to approach challenges with purpose.

By making this shift, you create space for expansive thinking, approaching situations with curiosity rather than anxiety. You start to prioritize proactive decisions aligned with your goals and values, seeing opportunities where you once saw obstacles. This transformation doesn't just enhance your experience—it changes your entire approach to life.

Section 4: Techniques for Shifting to Creation Mode

Transitioning to creation mode takes practice, especially if you're accustomed to high-stress situations. Here are some techniques to help reset your mindset and embrace a more open, balanced approach:

1.   Mindfulness and Meditation:
Mindfulness helps ground you in the present, reducing stress around past or future events. By observing your thoughts without judgment, you gain control over them instead of being controlled by them.

Practice: When stressed, focus on your breath. Count each inhale and exhale to anchor your mind in the present, easing your way out of survival mode.

2.   Deep Breathing Exercises:
Survival mode often leads to shallow breathing, which intensifies anxiety. Deep breathing activates your body's relaxation response, signaling that you're safe.

Practice: Try the 4-4-4 technique: inhale for four counts, hold for four, then exhale for four. Repeating this cycle calms your nervous system, making it easier to exit survival mode.

3.   Positive Visualization:
Imagining yourself in a peaceful or successful scenario counters negative thoughts common in survival mode. Visualization can foster creativity and a sense of possibility.

Practice: If you're nervous about an event, spend a few minutes visualizing it going well. Picture yourself calm and confident, training your mind to focus on positive outcomes.

4.   Engage in Creative Activities:
Creativity encourages exploration and self-expression, helping shift from defense to openness.

Practice: Set aside time for a creative hobby, like writing, drawing, or brainstorming. Letting go of rigid thinking helps foster creation mode.

5.   Exercise Regularly:

Physical activity releases endorphins, lifting your mood and reducing stress. Exercise helps release tension and clears your mind.

Practice: Incorporate regular physical activity into your routine, even if it's just a walk or stretching. Movement helps you reset mentally and physically, preparing you to approach challenges with an open mind.

6.   Set Purposeful Goals:

Clear, achievable goals focus your energy on what you want to create. Purposeful goals foster a sense of direction and growth.

Practice: Start with small goals aligned with your interests, such as a weekly creative activity. Focusing on what you want to build redirects your mind to creation mode.

Practical Example: Shifting to Creation Mode in Real Life

Consider preparing for an important presentation. In survival mode, your mind zooms in on potential mistakes, triggering anxiety and physical tension. This focus on what could go wrong heightens stress, causing overthinking and reducing confidence.

In contrast, a shift to creation mode changes your focus. Instead of fearing failure, you concentrate on your purpose—what you want to share and the impact you hope to make. You visualize success, picturing yourself speaking clearly and confidently, engaging with the audience. This mental rehearsal instills confidence, helping you approach the presentation with calm and purpose. In creation mode, the experience becomes about sharing ideas, not merely "getting it right," empowering you to be present and effective.

The Benefits of Living in Creation Mode

Living in creation mode opens a realm of possibilities, enabling you to thrive rather than simply survive. By shifting from a reactive, threat-focused mindset to one centered on growth, exploration, and connection, you unlock various benefits:

- **Enhanced Creativity:** A mind free from constant threat analysis has space for innovative thinking and problem-solving, welcoming possibilities over limitations.

- **Improved Mental Health:** Reduced stress supports mental well-being, lowering anxiety and burnout risks and promoting joy and fulfillment.

- **Stronger Relationships:** In creation mode, you're more open and present with others, fostering empathy and deeper connections.

- **Increased Resilience:** Viewing challenges as growth opportunities builds resilience, making setbacks feel like steps toward success and fostering optimism in adversity.

Conclusion

Embracing Creation Mode as a Way of Life

Shifting from survival mode to creation mode empowers you to live more fully and fearlessly. In creation mode, fear no longer dictates your decisions. Instead, you're driven by curiosity, excitement, and a sense of purpose. Techniques like mindfulness, creative activities, and setting purposeful goals can train your mind to focus on opportunities rather than dangers, allowing you to approach life with resilience and optimism.

The journey to living fearlessly isn't about eliminating fear, but learning to process it in ways that allow you to thrive. In the next chapter, we'll explore concrete steps for building a fearless mindset, helping you face challenges with courage, confidence, and clarity.

Reflection Exercise: Moving Toward Creation Mode

Consider a recent challenge that triggered your survival mode.

Write down:

1. What thoughts or feelings came up that put you in survival mode?

2. One action you can take next time to shift toward creation mode.

3. How you felt afterward, and what you learned from this experience.

Processing fear is about finding balance—allowing it to keep us safe without letting it limit our lives. By practicing creation mode, you open yourself to a life full of possibilities.

CHAPTER 4

PRACTICING FEARLESSNESS

Steps to a Bold and Courageous Life

Redefining Fearlessness

When you hear "fearless," what comes to mind?

Many think it implies a life without any fear—an existence untouched by worry or hesitation. But in reality, fear is a universal and natural response; even the most courageous individuals experience it. True fearlessness isn't about eradicating fear completely; it's about developing the ability to acknowledge fear, act in its presence, and gradually loosen its grip over your thoughts and actions.

Fear can serve as a guide, highlighting areas where growth is possible or signaling situations that require attention. Practicing fearlessness means recognizing the value in these signals while not allowing them to control your actions. It's about learning to navigate fear rather than avoiding it, building resilience with each experience.

In this chapter, we'll explore practical steps to help you cultivate resilience and confidence as you face your fears. These strategies are designed to make fear feel smaller and more manageable, empowering you to live with courage, conviction, and a deeper sense of freedom. By embracing these steps, you can expand your comfort zone, approach challenges with an open heart, and experience life without fear as a constant barrier.

Step 1: Understand Your Fears

The first step toward fearlessness is understanding the fears that hold you back. Fear can feel overwhelming, undefined, and even paralyzing, but by examining it closely, you can identify its root causes and dismantle it gradually. Understanding your fears reveals their origins, helping you see them as manageable challenges rather than immovable obstacles.

Break Fear Down into Specific Concerns

Instead of letting fear remain vague, break it into specific worries. Ask yourself: What exactly is causing my fear? This process can reveal that what seems like one overwhelming fear is actually made up of smaller, more manageable concerns.

Example: If you're anxious about a job interview, break it down: "I'm afraid of forgetting my responses" or "I'm worried about making a good impression." This allows you to prepare specifically—like practicing answers or researching company culture—making the fear smaller and boosting your confidence.

Identify the Underlying Beliefs

Often, specific fears are tied to limiting beliefs. For example, fear of public speaking may stem from the belief, "If I make a mistake, everyone will judge me." Recognizing these beliefs lets you question their validity and replace them with more empowering thoughts, such as "Everyone makes mistakes, and most people are understanding."

Why This Helps

Defining your fears lessens their power. Vague fears feel enormous, but when broken down, they become clear and actionable. This approach turns fear from an immobilizing force into a guide, helping you address each concern individually and build confidence along the way.

Step 2: Challenge Negative Thoughts

Fear often gains strength when fueled by negative thoughts. These automatic thoughts can convince you that you're incapable or destined to fail, limiting your potential. Practicing fearlessness requires challenging these thoughts and actively replacing them with more constructive perspectives.

Replace "I Can't" with "I Can Learn"

When fear tells you, "I can't do this," try reframing it as, "I can learn to do this." Fearlessness isn't about having all the answers; it's about trusting your capacity to grow.

Example: If public speaking scares you, replace "I can't do this" with "I'm learning to feel comfortable speaking in front of others." This mindset shift allows you to view challenges as growth opportunities.

Challenge Thoughts About Failure

Fear of failure often keeps us from taking important steps. When you feel anxious, question these thoughts: "Is this really true?" or "What evidence do I have?" Often, fears are based on assumptions, not facts.

Example: Instead of assuming the worst, try, "Even if I make mistakes, I'll learn from them." This perspective helps you see each experience as part of a learning process.

Why This Helps

Challenging negative thoughts empowers you to take more control of your mindset, building resilience and confidence. By replacing limiting beliefs with positive perspectives, you create an inner dialogue that supports growth, making it easier to act despite fear.

Step 3: Take Small, Courageous Steps

Fearlessness doesn't mean tackling your biggest fears all at once. Facing a massive fear head-on can feel overwhelming, so start by taking manageable steps that gradually build confidence.

Gradual Exposure to Fear
Begin with small steps and increase the challenge at your own pace.

Example: If public speaking makes you anxious, start by speaking alone, then with a friend. Gradually work up to a larger audience. Each step lessens the intensity of fear, making the next step easier.

Celebrate Each Small Win
Every time you step out of your comfort zone, celebrate it as a victory. For instance, if you're nervous about social events and attend one, acknowledge that progress.

Why This Helps
Taking small steps toward a goal builds resilience gradually. With each success, fear loses its grip, making larger challenges feel more achievable.

Step 4: Learn from Failure and Use It to Grow

Fear of failure is common and holds many people back. However, failure doesn't define your abilities—it's a chance to learn and improve.

Reframe Failure as Feedback
Instead of seeing failure as a setback, view it as valuable feedback.

Example: If you apply for a job and don't get it, reflect on what you can learn. Maybe it's an opportunity to refine your skills or better prepare for future interviews.

Look for Patterns in Failure
Repeated setbacks often indicate patterns worth exploring. Recognizing these patterns helps you make adjustments and progress toward your goals.

Example: If you frequently struggle to complete projects, examine why. Perhaps you take on too much or need to break tasks into smaller steps.

Why This Helps
Viewing failure as part of the learning journey reduces its intimidation factor. Instead of seeing setbacks as obstacles, you begin to view them as stepping stones toward growth, empowering you to move forward.

Step 5: Surround Yourself with Support

No one conquers fear alone. A strong support system makes a tremendous difference, offering encouragement and perspective.

Example: If you're nervous about a presentation, talk with a friend or mentor. They might offer advice or remind you of your strengths, which can reinforce your courage.

Why This Helps

Supportive people provide comfort and help you see your strengths, often becoming the extra push needed to face your fears. Their belief in you reinforces your self-confidence, shrinking fear and making it easier to act boldly.

Step 6: Practice Self-Compassion

Fearlessness isn't about suppressing feelings; it's about treating yourself with kindness and understanding. Self-compassion means extending the same warmth and patience to yourself that you would to a friend, fostering resilience and a nurturing inner environment.

Forgive Yourself for Mistakes

Mistakes are part of growth. When setbacks occur, avoid self-criticism; instead, remind yourself that everyone makes mistakes.

Example: If you freeze during a presentation, say, "This happens to everyone. I can learn from this and improve." Self-compassion helps you let go of self-judgment and maintain a growth-oriented perspective.

Acknowledge Efforts, Not Just Results
Fearlessness is about effort and perseverance, not perfection. Recognize the courage it took to face a challenge, regardless of the outcome.

Example: After a difficult day, remind yourself, "I did my best today, and that's enough." Valuing your efforts helps prevent discouragement.

Why Self-Compassion Helps
Self-compassion creates a supportive inner voice that fosters growth. By replacing harsh self-criticism with kindness, you reduce the pressure of self-evaluation, allowing you to approach challenges with resilience. This mindset enables authentic growth by making it safe to take risks and face fears.

Conclusion

Embracing Fearlessness Every Day

Living fearlessly doesn't mean fear will disappear; it means facing life with courage, even in the presence of fear. By understanding your fears, challenging negative thoughts, taking small steps, learning from setbacks, building a support system, and practicing self-compassion, you cultivate resilience and confidence.

Each small step toward fearlessness opens new possibilities, bringing you closer to a life of purpose, fulfillment, and joy.

Reflection Exercise: Building Fearlessness

Identify a fear that you'd like to work on overcoming.

Write down:

1. One small step you can take toward facing this fear.

2. A positive thought or phrase to replace negative self-talk when fear arises.

3. One person you can share your goal with for support.

Each action you take toward fearlessness builds confidence and helps you step into the life you want. Embrace this moment as a powerful step on your journey from fearful to fearless.

CHAPTER 5

FROM FEARFUL TO FEARLESS

Embracing Fear as a Catalyst for Growth

Introduction:
The Journey from Fearful to Fearless

As we conclude this book, take a moment to reflect on the transformative journey you've just completed. Transitioning from a fear-driven life to one defined by courage and resilience is no small feat. Each chapter has delved into different facets of fear—its origins, impacts, and, most importantly, the ways to turn it into a source of strength.

Fear isn't something to eradicate; instead, it's something to understand, accept, and manage. Practicing fearlessness doesn't mean living without fear—it's about responding to it in ways that unlock growth, resilience, and joy.

In this final chapter, we'll revisit key insights from this journey and explore how you can continue using fear as a tool for personal growth.

Section 1: Acknowledging Fear as a Natural Part of Life

Fear is a universal experience, and our response to it defines our ability to live freely. The first step toward a fearless life is acknowledging our fears openly. Though it may sound simple, many people spend years avoiding or suppressing fears, hoping they'll fade on their own. Yet, ignored fears often grow stronger, subtly influencing our thoughts, choices, and actions. Acknowledgment allows us to bring fears out of the shadows and see them for what they are—emotional responses, not unavoidable limitations.

Example: Facing the Fear of Difficult Conversations

Imagine you've been postponing a difficult conversation with a friend or loved one, hoping the issue will resolve itself. But avoiding the issue usually only amplifies anxiety. By acknowledging the fear and choosing to face it, you take the first step toward resolution and growth. You might tell yourself, "I'm afraid of how this might go, but avoiding it holds me back from a deeper connection." This acknowledgment empowers you to approach the situation with courage and commitment.

Reflection: Recognizing the Origins of Fear

Ask yourself: Where does this fear come from? Is it rooted in a fear of rejection, failure, vulnerability, or uncertainty? Understanding the origin of our fears provides clarity, allowing us to respond in ways aligned with our values, rather than letting fear control our actions. For example, the fear of rejection may stem from past experiences, while the fear of failure could arise from perfectionism. Recognizing these origins helps us not only address the fear but also challenge the beliefs reinforcing it.

Moving Beyond Fear with Self-Compassion

As you begin confronting your fears, practicing self-compassion is essential. Recognize that fear is a natural response shared by all. Treat yourself kindly, viewing each step forward as a courageous act. Self-compassion allows you to approach fear with patience, making it easier to take gradual steps without the added burden of self-judgment.

By acknowledging, understanding, and approaching fear with self-compassion, you can transform it into an opportunity for growth, enabling you to make choices aligned with your true self and move forward confidently.

Section 2: Addressing Internal Conflicts – Aligning with Your True Self

Beyond acknowledging fear, it's vital to address internal conflicts that fuel anxiety. Internal conflict arises when our actions misalign with our core values, passions, or desires. Often, we make choices based on others' expectations or a fear of disappointing people, rather than following our own path.

Living in Alignment with Your True Self
Living in alignment with your true self reduces internal conflict, creating a sense of peace and purpose. For example, if you're in a job that doesn't fulfill you but stay because it feels safe or expected, this misalignment can lead to dissatisfaction. Your heart may yearn for something more meaningful, yet fear of the unknown holds you back. Addressing this conflict means recognizing your desire for purpose and making decisions aligned with your values, even if it involves uncertainty.

Example: Pursuing a Passion Despite Fear

Let's say you've dreamed of starting your own business, but the fear of failure stops you. While the security of a steady job is comforting, you feel a deep, unfulfilled desire to create or innovate. Addressing this conflict could mean starting small by working on your passion on the side or setting achievable goals. Aligning with your true self helps diminish fear's grip, leading to a more authentic life.

Section 3: Moving from Survival Mode to Creation Mode

One transformative shift from fearful to fearless is moving from survival mode—a reactive, fear-driven state—to creation mode, where growth, creativity, and possibility flourish. In survival mode, we're constantly on guard for threats, which can protect us short-term but confines us, limiting our capacity to connect meaningfully, think freely, and pursue dreams with intention.

Creation mode, however, allows us to approach life with openness, focusing on growth. For instance, if you're starting a new project or relationship, survival mode might dwell on potential risks: "What if I fail? What if I'm judged?" But in creation mode, your focus shifts to possibilities: "What can I learn? How might this experience enrich my life?" This mindset encourages you to lean into the unknown with curiosity, engaging more fully with life.

In creation mode, fear is replaced by excitement for what's possible. You see challenges as growth opportunities, making it easier to take risks, dream big, and live aligned with your values. Creation mode fosters inner calm, as energy is directed toward building rather than defending. Instead of exhausting yourself with "what ifs" focused on failure, you ask, "What if this leads to something amazing?"

Section 4: Practical Steps for Shifting into Creation Mode

1.   Visualization

Each morning, spend a few minutes visualizing yourself pursuing your goals with excitement instead of fear. Picture scenarios where you move confidently toward your ambitions and handle setbacks as learning opportunities. This practice helps set a positive tone for your day, keeping you focused on growth rather than on avoiding risks.

2.   Setting Growth Goals

Rather than setting goals solely to avoid failure, establish ones that emphasize learning and exploration. Creation mode thrives on curiosity and boundary-pushing. Set intentions to explore new skills or test your abilities, even if not perfectly. This shift encourages a mindset where each challenge becomes a chance to expand.

3.   Practicing Fearlessness – Building Resilience Through Action

Living fearlessly means acting despite fear. Throughout this book, we've explored strategies for challenging negative thoughts, taking courageous steps, learning from setbacks, and building support networks. Practicing fearlessness involves gradually stepping out of your comfort zone. Each action reinforces your belief in your ability, gradually transforming fear into empowerment.

Section 5: Turning Fear into a Tool for Growth

A powerful shift in moving from fearful to fearless is realizing fear can serve as a growth catalyst. Fear often arises as we approach our comfort zone's edge, signaling moments ripe for transformation. Instead of seeing fear as a barrier, reframe it as a guide that highlights areas for self-improvement.

Example: Fear of Career Change as Growth Opportunity

If contemplating a career change but held back by fear, consider it a signal you're ready for a new phase. Embracing this fear can lead to profound self-discovery, helping you tap into strengths and resilience. The challenges of transition push you to develop skills, expand your network, and find purpose—all growth components.

Reflection: Viewing Fear as a Guide

When fear arises, pause and ask what it's guiding you toward. Fear often accompanies experiences with the most potential for transformation. Embracing fear reframes it from a roadblock to a guide, helping you enter new possibilities with courage.

Conclusion

The Endless Possibilities of a Fearless Life

The journey from fearful to fearless is lifelong. While fear will always be present, it doesn't have to control you. By acknowledging fear, aligning with your true self, embracing creation mode, and taking action despite fear, you open yourself to endless possibilities. Trust yourself, commit to this journey, and remember that each step forward brings you closer to a life rich with purpose and potential. Here's to a fearless, fulfilled, and courageous life.

Fear is part of our journey, and every time we face it, we grow stronger. Embrace this chapter as a celebration of how far you've come—and as a reminder of the limitless potential that lies ahead.

ABOUT THE AUTHOR

Mike Jensen II is a Life Performance Coach with over 12 years of experience helping individuals achieve the greatest performance of their lives and live up to their potential. He holds several certifications in Energy Leadership, Mental Toughness Training, Professional Coaching, and the Science of Happiness. Mike writes a daily short blog on various social media platforms under MBR3 Coaching, which has been updated every day for over eight years without fail. His blog focuses on encouraging others to think outside the box, recognize the abundance around them, and choose a different way to live.

When he's not writing or blogging, Mike is coaching clients all over the world. In his personal time, he enjoys spending time with his amazing wife, family, and especially his grandchildren. Although Mike has lived all over the United States, he always returns to Ottawa, Kansas, a small town he loves for its smallness, slowness, and quietness.

Mike has dedicated his life to serving others, helping them find sustainable happiness and live up to their potential. He believes that everyone has a purpose and unlimited potential.

ABOUT THE PUBLISHER

Dear Reader,

As you hold this remarkable book in your hands, we want to express our heartfelt gratitude for becoming a part of the Live Life Happy Community of readers. Your curiosity and thirst for knowledge fuel our passion for publishing meaningful non-fiction works.

At Live Life Happy Publishing, our mission is rooted in bringing forth literature that not only entertains but uplifts, supports, and nourishes the soul. We firmly believe that books have the power to transform lives, to ignite passions, and to spread joy far and wide.

Behind every word, every chapter, lies the dedication of our authors who pour their hearts and souls into their craft. Their ultimate aim? To touch your life in profound ways, to inspire, and to leave an indelible mark on your journey.

Your role in this journey is invaluable; by sharing your thoughts through reviews, spreading the word to others, or reaching out to the authors themselves, you become an integral part of sparking transformation in countless lives, igniting a ripple effect of joy and enlightenment.

And if, perchance, you or someone you know has dreams of writing, of sharing a message, or of unleashing a powerful story unto the world, know that Live Life Happy Publishing stands ready to guide you. Our doors are open, our ears attuned, and our hearts eager to hear your message.

So, dear reader, let us, continue to spread the power of literature, one page at a time. Reach out, share, and most importantly, never underestimate the power of your message to touch lives.

With warmest regards,

LiveLifeHappyPublishing.com

P.S. Remember, books change lives. Whose life will you touch with yours?

LiveLifeHappy
Publishing

www.ingramcontent.com/pod-product-compliance
Lightning Source LLC
LaVergne TN
LVHW051817080426
835513LV00017B/1993